"Joseph the Dreamer"
Published by John Eck
PO Box 373
Olympia Fields, IL 60461
www.johneckhardt.global

This book or parts thereof may not be reproduced in any form, stored in a retrieval system, or transmitted in any form by any means—electronic, mechanical, photocopy, recording, or otherwise—without prior written permission of the publisher, except as provided by United States of America copyright law.

Unless otherwise noted, all Scripture quotations are taken from the King James Version of the Bible. Scripture quotations marked "amp" are from the Amplified Bible. Copyright © 1954, 1958, 1962, 1964, 1965, 1987 by The Lockman Foundation. Used by permission.

Scripture quotations marked ampc are from the Amplified Bible, Classic Edition. Copyright © 1954, 1958, 1962, 1964, 1965, 1987 by The Lockman Foundation. Used by permission.

Scripture quotations marked "asv" are from the American Standard Bible."

"Scripture quotations marked "gnt" are from the Good News Translation® (Today's English Version, Second Edition) Copyright © 1992 American Bible Society. All rights reserved.

Scripture quotations marked nasb are from the New American Standard Bible, copyright © 1960, 1962, 1963, 1968, 1971, 1972, 1973, 1975, 1977,

1995 by The Lockman Foundation. Used by permission. (www.Lockman.org)
Scripture quotations marked niv are taken from the Holy Bible, New International Version®, NIV®. Copyright © 1973, 1978, 1984, 2011 by Biblica, Inc.™ Used by permission of Zondervan. All rights reserved worldwide. www.zondervan.com The "NIV" and "New International Version" are trademarks registered in the United States Patent and Trademark Office by Biblica, Inc.™

Copyright © 2020 by John Eckhardt
All rights reserved
Visit the author's website at
www.johneckhardt.global

Table of Contents

Introduction   1
Joseph The Dreamer   5
Envy (Jealousy) and Cruelty   7
Hatred and Murder   9
Flesh Versus Spirit   12
Spirits of Bondage and Hurt   15
Prosperity and Favor   18
The Fear of the Lord   21
Integrity   23
Lies   25
Favor In Prison   27
Mercy   28
Dream Interpretation   32
Pharaoh's Dreams   35
Joseph's Counsel   39
Promotion   41
Authority And Wisdom   43
Famine   46
Brokenness, Repentance, Forgiveness and Reconcili-
ation   49
Jacob Before Pharaoh   57
Joseph's Final Words to His Brethren   61
The Word of the Lord Tested Him   65
Manasseh and Ephraim   67
Legacy and Blessings   68
Lessons from the Life of Joseph   70

Introduction

I love the story of Joseph. His story speaks of family, hurt, rejection, betrayal, jealousy, affliction, dreaming, destiny, overcoming, righteousness, grace, gifting, integrity, favor, humility, suffering, patience, testing, mercy, promotion, honor, reconciliation, deliverance, wisdom, understanding, forgiveness, legacy, purpose, protection, government, authority, power, influence, prominence, counsel, double portion, and prosperity.

Let's look first at the Joseph story, which begins thus:

Genesis 30:23-25
And she conceived, and bare a son; and said, God hath taken away my reproach:
And she called his name Joseph; and said, The Lord shall add to me another son.
And it came to pass, when Rachel had born Joseph, that Jacob said unto Laban, Send me away, that I may go unto mine own place, and to my country.

It was the birth of Joseph that prompted Jacob to leave Laban's house and return to his own land. Rachel was the beloved wife of Jacob. She was barren. Joseph's birth was a picture of the miraculous. We'll see throughout this book that Joseph is a type of a Christ. Jesus was born of a virgin - a miraculous birth. Jacob favored Joseph. The fact that he was born so unexpectedly, in his old age, likely contributed to him loving Joseph so much. Joseph is the favored son, He is a type of Christ the favored son (Luke 2:52). Typology is a form of symbolism that is prophetic. In Old Testament typology, there are people and objects that foreshadow what is yet to happen or someone (most often Jesus) who is yet to come. Joseph is clearly seen as a type of Jesus throughout his life

Genesis 37:2
These are the generations of Jacob. Joseph, being seventeen years old, was feeding the flock with his brethren; and the lad was with the sons of Bilhah, and with the sons of Zilpah, his father's wives: and Joseph brought unto his father their evil report.

Joseph's story is one of the most compelling in scripture. Fourteen chapters in the book of Genesis tell his story. The reason so many verses in scripture speak of Joseph's life is because there are numerous lessons we can learn by studying him.

Joseph is also a type of Christ. His rejection and suffering prefigure the rejection and suffering of Christ by his brethren. Joseph's brethren envied him. Jesus was envied by the religious leaders of his day. Joseph became Israel's deliverer. Christ was Israel's deliverer. Joseph was falsely accused and put in prison. Jesus was falsely accused and taken to judgment. Joseph was sold for twenty pieces of silver. Jesus was sold for thirty pieces of silver. Joseph was exalted to a place of authority. Jesus was exalted as the king of kings.

When we find significant time spent on an Old Testament figure, particularly one who is found to be in God's favor, we most often find someone who is pointing figuratively to the Messiah to come. This is particularly true for Joseph and David, whom Jewish authorities for centuries even before Christ's first coming understood to be two of the most significant pictures of the Messiah to come: "HaMashiach ben Josef" and "HaMashiach ben David"—"The Messiah the Son of Joseph" and "The Messiah the Son of David". We can see both suffering and ruling in the life of David. We can also see both suffering and ruling in the life of Joseph.

Samuel Emadi states, "Moses gives Joseph more time in Genesis than he does any other character—a striking fact given the significance of Genesis's other main characters: Adam, Noah, and the patriarchs Abraham, Isaac, and Jacob. This prominence is even more striking considering the apparent insignificance of Joseph in the rest of Scripture. Joseph's story is the story of the whole Bible. It's the story of glory through suffering, exaltation through humiliation. It's the story of the cross and the crown." (What the Joseph Story is Really about by Samuel Emadi, thegospelcoalition.org)

God's promise to Abraham that his seed would bless all nations can be seen in a figure through Joseph. The ultimate fulfillment is Christ, but Joseph is raised up in his generation to bless the surrounding nations by providing them corn. Joseph becomes the deliverer of his generation. The Messianic prophecy to Judah that his brethren would bow to him (fulfilled in Christ) is typified by Joseph's brethren having to bow to him.

Joseph's problems with his brethren begins with his fathers favoritism. Israel loved Joseph more than all of his brethren because he was the son of his old age. His brethren hated him as a result. Joseph also reported their bad behavior to his father, which did not endear him to his brethren.

Genesis 37:3-4

Now Israel loved Joseph more than all his children, because he was the son of his old age: and he made him a coat of many colours.

And when his brethren saw that their father loved him more than all his brethren, they hated him, and could not speak peaceably unto him.

Israel made Joseph a coat of many colors. The coat of many colors is royal garb. Joseph's garment is a prophetic symbol of his eventual rule in Egypt.

Joseph The Dreamer

Joseph's brethren hated him even more because of his dreams.

Genesis 37:5-8

And Joseph dreamed a dream, and he told it his brethren: and they hated him yet the more.

And he said unto them, Hear, I pray you, this dream which I have dreamed:

For, behold, we were binding sheaves in the field, and, lo, my sheaf arose, and also stood upright; and, behold, your sheaves stood round about, and made obeisance to my sheaf.

And his brethren said to him, Shalt thou indeed reign over us? or shalt thou indeed have dominion over us? And they hated him yet the more for his dreams, and for his words.

His brethren also envied him because of his dreams, but his father observed them.

Genesis 37:9-11

And he dreamed yet another dream, and told it his brethren, and said, Behold, I have dreamed a dream more; and, behold, the sun and the moon and the eleven stars made obeisance to me.

And he told it to his father, and to his brethren: and his father rebuked him, and said unto him, What is this dream that thou hast dreamed? Shall I and thy mother and thy brethren indeed come to bow down ourselves to thee to the earth?

And his brethren envied him; but his father observed the saying.

Joseph's dreams were showing him the future. He would rule over his brethren, although he was the youngest. This was more than his brethren could handle and they began to envy him.

Genesis 37:19-20

And they said one to another, Behold, this dreamer cometh.

Come now therefore, and let us slay him, and cast him into some pit, and we will say, Some evil beast hath devoured him: and we shall see what will become of his dreams

Joseph dreamed that the stars and moon would bow to him. Joseph's dreams provoked his brothers. They could not conceive that their younger brother would rule over them. They hated his dreams. They were offended by his dreams. Joseph's dreams revealed what was inside of them. Joseph could not have imagined where his dreams would take him. The destiny and future of his family was foretold by his dreams.

Envy (Jealousy) and Cruelty

One of the lessons we learn from the story is the destructive nature of envy and jealousy.

Genesis 37:11
*And his brethren **envied** him; but his father observed the saying.*

Proverbs 27:4
*Wrath is cruel, and anger is outrageous; but who is able to stand before **envy**?*

Song of Solomon 8:6
*Set me as a seal upon thine heart, as a seal upon thine arm: for love is strong as death; **jealousy** is cruel as the grave: the coals thereof are coals of fire, which hath a most vehement flame.*

These verses tell us that envy (jealousy) is worse than wrath and anger, and is as cruel as the grave. Envy would be the motive behind their mistreatment of Joseph. Envy is defined as a feeling of discontented or resentful longing aroused by someone else's possessions, qualities, or luck. Envy drives men to commit cruel acts. Joseph was not celebrated by his brethren, instead he was hated and despised by them. They did not possess the character and qualities of Joseph.

7

They would eventually sell their brother into slavery. What a cruel act.

Matthew 27:18
*For he knew that for **envy** they had delivered him.*

Mark 15:10
*For he knew that the chief priests had delivered him for **envy**.*

Envy is rottenness to the bones. Envy opens the door for spirits of sickness and infirmity. Envy is the opposite of a sound heart.

Proverbs 14:30
*A sound heart is the life of the flesh: but **envy** the rottenness of the bones.*

Hatred and Murder

Joseph and his dreams were rejected by his brothers. His dreams caused his brothers to hate him even more. Rejection is a common issue with many. It is painful, especially from your brothers.

Genesis 37:8

*And his brethren said to him, Shalt thou indeed reign over us? or shalt thou indeed have dominion over us? And they hated him yet the more for his **dreams**, and for his words.*

Hatred is akin to murder (1 John 3:15). Satan is a murderer (John 8:44). The original plan was to kill Joseph.

Genesis 37:20-22

Come now therefore, and let us slay him, and cast him into some pit, and we will say, Some evil beast hath devoured him: and we shall see what will become of his dreams.

And Reuben heard it, and he delivered him out of their hands; and said, Let us not kill him.

And Reuben said unto them, Shed no blood, but cast him into this pit that is in the wilderness, and lay no hand upon him; that he might rid him out of their hands, to deliver him to his father again.

Satan is a murderer. Joseph's brothers were being controlled by the devil. Reuben saved Joseph's life. God would not allow the enemy to kill Joseph.

This was more than a hatred of Joseph. This was a hatred for the plan of God. Joseph's dreams were from God. Jesus was also hated (John 15:25). Jesus was murdered (Acts 7:52)

Joseph was stripped of his coat. His brethren obviously hated what his coat represented. Jesus was also stripped of his coat (John 19:23). Joseph's coat would later be dipped in blood and given to his father. Jesus coat was also dipped in blood (Rev. 19:13).

Genesis 37:23
And it came to pass, when Joseph was come unto his brethren, that they stript Joseph out of his coat, his coat of many colours that was on him;

Jacob's prophecy over Joseph likens this hatred to archers shooting arrows. Arrows are deadly and Joseph was grieved by this hatred.

Genesis 49:22-23
Joseph is a fruitful bough, even a fruitful bough by a well; whose branches run over the wall:
The archers have sorely grieved him, and shot at him, and hated him:
The Amplified version says,

"The [skilled] archers have bitterly attacked and provoked him; They have shot [at him] and harassed him.

The CEB Translation says,
"They attacked him fiercely and fired arrows; the archers attacked him furiously."

Flesh Versus Spirit

Joseph's story reveals much about dysfunctional families and family dynamics.

Jacob had two wives. He loved Rachel, but was deceived by his father-in-law into marrying Leah. Leah was hated, but God opened her womb. Rachel's womb was closed.

There was a rivalry between the two sisters to please Jacob. This rivalry included the use of concubines to have children. God eventually opened Rachel's womb and she had Joseph. Joseph became Jacob's favorite son.

The problem in this family is compounded by the fact that Jacob's sons are born to four different women. Joseph's brethren were probably resentful of the fact that Jacob loved Rachel and favored Joseph. Before we are too hard on Jacob for favoring Joseph, we need to consider that Jacob was tricked into marrying Leah by his unscrupulous uncle Laban. Jacob loved Rachel, but she was barren. God opened Leah's womb because she was hated. Leah was caught in the middle of her fathers's dealings with Jacob.

Proverbs 17:17
A friend loveth at all times, and a brother is born for adversity.

The scriptures speak of the troubles between Jacob and Esau. We now see the troubles between Joseph and his brothers. It is a picture of the flesh versus the spirit. The flesh is envious, jealous, and hateful. The spirit is loving, kind, and forgiving. The flesh always fights and persecutes the spirit.

Galatians 4:29

*But as then he that was born after the **flesh persecuted** him that was born after the Spirit, even so it is now.*

This is a battle that all of us will have to fight and win. Your flesh will war against your spirit and desire to control it. Your spirit must gain the ascendency over your flesh. You cannot allow your flesh to dominate your life.

In the life of the brothers of Joseph we can see the works of the flesh.

Galatians 5:19-21

Now the works of the flesh are manifest, which are these; Adultery, fornication, uncleanness, lasciviousness, Idolatry, witchcraft, hatred, variance, emulations, wrath, strife, seditions, heresies, Envyings, murders, drunkenness, revellings, and such like: of the which I tell you before, as I have also told you in time past, that they which do such things shall not inherit the kingdom of God.

In the life of Joseph we can see the fruits of the Spirit.

Galatians 5:22-23
But the fruit of the Spirit is love, joy, peace, long-suffering, gentleness, goodness, faith, Meekness, temperance: against such there is no law.

Spirits of Bondage and Hurt

Joseph was sold by his brothers to Midianite merchantmen. The Midianites were descendents of Midian who was the son of one of Abraham's wives (Keturah). Midian was a Grand Uncle of Joseph. In other words someone related to Joseph, other than his brethren, carried him into Egypt.

Genesis 37:28
Then there passed by Midianites merchantmen; and they drew and lifted up Joseph out of the pit, and sold Joseph to the Ishmeelites for twenty pieces of silver: and they brought Joseph into Egypt.

Genesis 37:36
And the Midianites sold him into Egypt unto Potiphar, an officer of Pharaoh's, and captain of the guard.

Joseph is being traded, sold, and brought into Egypt by his family. Slavery is the spirit of bondage. The Psalmist tells us that Joseph was hurt by his chains.

Psalm 105:17-18
He sent a man before them, even Joseph, who was sold for a servant
Whose feet they hurt with fetters: he was laid in iron:

These verses also tell us that Joseph was sent into Egypt. God was using their envy and hatred to send Joseph before them. God knew that they would eventually follow.

I cannot imagine how much pain and hurt this caused Joseph. These were his older brothers. He was now separated from his family and his beloved father Jacob. He would not see them or know their well being for years to come.

Most people have to overcome hurt and rejection at some point in their life. Hurt is a common problem for many, often coming from those who are family. This hurt goes even deeper because it comes from the people who should protect and love us.

Joseph was laid in iron. This is a symbol of bondage and restraint. He was no longer a free man. His life was now subject unto his owners. Man was not intended to live in bondage as there is a desire for freedom in every person.

God would eventually deliver Joseph from his chains and bondage. Joseph's story is one of deliverance. God is willing and able to deliver. We can all be delivered from our chains and fetters.

How often did Joseph think of his family while in Egypt? How often did he pray for freedom? How often did he pray to be brought back to his family? How often did he cry while away? How often did his brothers think of him after they did such a cruel act? How often did his father cry after losing his favorite son? There is so much hurt and pain in this story.

Israel would come to be enslaved in Egypt. Joseph's brethren sold him as a slave and their descendants would end up in slavery. It seems as if this would be the horrible result of their crime. They could have never imagined the results of their act. God would eventually use their act to bring glory to his name with a mighty deliverance from Pharaoh.

Prosperity and Favor

<u>Genesis 39:1-4</u>

And Joseph was brought down to Egypt; and Potiphar, an officer of Pharaoh, captain of the guard, an Egyptian, bought him of the hands of the Ishmeelites, which had brought him down thither.

And the Lord was with Joseph, and he was a prosperous man; and he was in the house of his master the Egyptian.

And his master saw that the Lord was with him, and that the Lord made all that he did to prosper in his hand.

And Joseph found grace in his sight, and he served him: and he made him overseer over his house, and all that he had he put into his hand.

Joseph becomes a servant. He is a type of the greatest servant: Jesus Christ. This is a picture of the kingdom. The greatest is a servant in the kingdom.

Joseph is called a prosperous man. The word prosperous is the Hebrew word "Tsalach". It means to rush, to advance, to make progress, to succeed, and to be profitable.

Other translations say Joseph found "favor" in his master's sight. Prosperity and favor are linked. Favor can be defined as someone, including God, who willingly uses their power, influence, authority, position, or resources on your behalf. Potiphar saw that everything Joseph did prospered. Potiphar then made Joseph overseer over his house.

Joseph in Potiphar's house is a picture of humility. Joseph finds himself in a low place. Favor is connected to humility. God gives grace (favor) to the humble. It is in this place of humility that Joseph serves his master.

There are many examples in the word of God that reveal serving as a key to promotion. Joshua served Moses. Samuel served Eli. Elisha served Elijah. David served Saul.

Joseph learns to be a steward and a servant in Potiphar's house. He would eventually be a steward for Pharaoh over all of Egypt. Joseph is in training for reigning.

Joseph is then made overseer over Potiphar's house. Favor is a key to promotion. Joseph is being promoted although he is in a strange land. Favor brings promotion, Joseph would always find promotion at the lowest points in his life.

The LORD blessed Potiphar's house for Joseph's sake. Potiphar turned his entire household over to Joseph's keeping. Joseph becomes the steward of Potiphar's possessions.

Genesis 39:5-6

And it came to pass from the time that he had made him overseer in his house, and over all that he had, that the Lord blessed the Egyptian's house for Joseph's sake; and the blessing of the Lord was upon all that he had in the house, and in the field. And he left all that he had in Joseph's hand; and he knew not ought he had, save the bread which he did eat. And Joseph was a goodly person, and well favoured.

We can learn the lessons of stewardship, service, trust, and humility from this part of Joseph's life. Potiphar trusted Joseph and saw integrity in him. Joesph served Potiphar. Humility and serving are keys to promotion. Some people want to be promoted without serving, but serving is often a prerequisite to promotion.

Joseph was also goodly and well favored. He was attractive in form and appearance. This would eventually cause a problem with Potiphar's wife. Things were going well for Joseph until his problem with his master's wife.

The Fear of the Lord

Genesis 39:7-9

And it came to pass after these things, that his master's wife cast her eyes upon Joseph; and she said, Lie with me.

But he refused, and said unto his master's wife, Behold, my master wotteth not what is with me in the house, and he hath committed all that he hath to my hand;

There is none greater in this house than I; neither hath he kept back any thing from me but thee, because thou art his wife: how then can I do this great wickedness, and sin against God?

Joseph resisted the advances of Potiphar's wife. Joseph had the fear of the LORD. This is one of the most important qualities we can possess. Humility and the fear of the a Lord bring riches, honor, and life.

Proverbs 22:4

*By **humility** and the **fear of the Lord** are riches, and honour, and life.*

The fear of the a Lord causes men to hate evil and depart from it.

Proverbs 3:7

*Be not wise in thine own eyes: **fear the Lord**, and depart from evil.*

Proverbs 8:13
*The **fear of the Lord** is to hate evil: pride, and arrogancy, and the evil way, and the froward mouth, do I hate.*

The fear of the Lord is the beginning of wisdom. It breaks poverty and lack.

Proverbs 9:10
*The **fear of the Lord** is the beginning of wisdom: and the knowledge of the holy is understanding.*

Psalm 34:9
*O **fear the Lord**, ye his saints: for there is no want to them that fear him.*

Psalm 111:10
*The **fear of the Lord** is the beginning of wisdom: a good understanding have all they that do his commandments: his praise endureth for ever.*

This is also a lesson in resisting temptation. Temptation will come to those who have a dream and a destiny. Joseph had to overcome this temptation before he would be promoted to honor.

Integrity

Joseph had integrity. Integrity is defined as
the quality of being honest and having strong
moral principles; moral uprightness. completeness.
The Hebrew Word for integrity means fullness, per-
fection, innocence, and simplicity. Integrity also
means prosperity. Integrity will guide you.

Proverbs 11:3
*The **integrity** of the upright shall guide them: but
the perverseness of transgressors shall destroy
them.*

Integrity will preserve you.

Psalm 25:21
*Let **integrity** and uprightness preserve me; for I
wait on thee.*

God upholds those with integrity.

Psalm 41:12
*And as for me, thou upholdest me in mine
integrity, and settest me before thy face for ever.*

Integrity is the fruit of righteousness.

Proverbs 20:7
*The just man walketh in his **integrity**: his children
are blessed after him.*

"Integrity stems from the Latin word 'integer' which means whole and complete. So integrity requires an inner sense of 'wholeness' and consistency of character. When you are in integrity, people should be able to visibly see it through your actions, words, decisions, methods, and outcomes. When you are 'whole' and consistent, there is only one you. You bring that same you wherever you are, regardless of the circumstance. You don't leave parts of yourself behind. You don't have a 'work you,' a 'family you,' and a 'social you.' You are YOU all the time." (So-Young Kang)

Integrity means to be consistently righteous. It also means to be level and straight. It means to live without compromise.

Isaiah 26:7
The way of the [consistently] righteous (those living in moral and spiritual rectitude in every area and relationship of their lives) is level and straight; You, O [Lord], Who are upright, direct aright and make level the path of the [uncompromisingly] just and righteous. (Amplified Classic)

Lies

Genesis 39:12-14
And she caught him by his garment, saying, Lie with me: and he left his garment in her hand, and fled, and got him out.

And it came to pass, when she saw that he had left his garment in her hand, and was fled forth,

That she called unto the men of her house, and spake unto them, saying, See, he hath brought in an Hebrew unto us to mock us; he came in unto me to lie with me, and I cried with a loud voice:

Psalm 120:2
*Deliver my soul, O Lord, from **lying** lips, and from a deceitful tongue.*

Joseph becomes the victim of a lie. God hates the lying tongue (Prov. 6:17). The lying tongue is one of the most destructive things known to man. It can destroy lives and reputations.

This lie would put Joseph in prison. This lie would cause Joseph immeasurable pain. There are few things worse than false accusation. This was compounded by the fact that a Joseph was a servant and had no recourse to counter this lie. This lie would put Joseph in the lowest place of his life. This lie would put an innocent man in prison. It was an attack on his integrity. Lying is the nature of the devil (John 8:44); Satan is an accuser (Rev. 12:10).

Joseph's brethren lied to their father concerning Joseph in an attempt to cover up their sin. This lie also caused Jacob much grief, believing that Joseph was dead.

Lord deliver us from lies and the lying tongue. Let every lying tongue be silenced and overturned. Let every lie of the enemy be exposed and exposed. Let no lie stop our destiny and purpose from coming to pass.

Favor In Prison

Genesis 39:20-23

And Joseph's master took him, and put him into the prison, a place where the king's prisoners were bound: and he was there in the prison.

But the Lord was with Joseph, and shewed him mercy, and gave him favour in the sight of the keeper of the prison.

And the keeper of the prison committed to Joseph's hand all the prisoners that were in the prison; and whatsoever they did there, he was the doer of it.

The keeper of the prison looked not to any thing that was under his hand; because the Lord was with him, and that which he did, the Lord made it to prosper.

Joseph is put in prison, but he is strategically placed among the king's prisoners. It is possible that Potiphar did not believe the accusation, but placed him in prison because of his wife. The Lord was with Joseph. This again is a definition of prosperity. Joseph will prosper in prison. Joseph is placed in charge of all the prisoners, operating in authority even while in prison.

We also see another example of favor while in prison. God gives Joseph favor with the jailor even as he had favor with Potiphar. God favored Joseph because of his righteousness and integrity.

Mercy

But the Lord was with Joseph, and shewed him mercy, and gave him favour in the sight of the keeper of the prison. (Gen. 39:21)

God had mercy on Joseph. Mercy is lovingkindness. Lovingkindness is tender and benevolent affection. God's mercy was a key to Joseph's survival and eventual deliverance.

Mercy is also stedfast love. Mercy is the Hebrew word "CHESED", meaning goodness, kindness, and faithfulness. God is faithful to Joseph and would not forsake him, even in the prison.

Mercy is connected to life, righteousness, and honor.

Proverbs 21:21
*He that followeth after righteousness and **mercy** findeth life, righteousness, and honour.*

Mercy is connected to goodness. Joseph experienced God's goodness while in prison.

Psalm 23:6
*Surely goodness and **mercy** shall follow me all the days of my life: and I will dwell in the house of the Lord for ever.*

Mercy is connected to trusting God. Joseph had to trust a God in the midst of his trouble.

Psalm 32:10
Many sorrows shall be to the wicked: but he that trusteth in the Lord, **mercy** shall compass him about.

God's mercy is stedfast. God's mercy gave Joseph victory over his enemies.

Psalm 59:10 (AMP)
My God in His [steadfast] lovingkindness will meet me;
God will let me look triumphantly on my enemies [who lie in wait for me].

Joseph in prison is a picture of the lowest hell. God's mercy was manifested in Joseph's worst time.

Psalm 86:13
For great is thy **mercy** toward me: and thou hast delivered my soul from the lowest hell.

Mercy is connected to the fear of the Lord. Mercy is extended to those who fear God. We have already looked at Joseph's fear of the LORD.

Psalm 103:11

*For as the heaven is high above the earth, so great is his **mercy** toward them that fear him.*

Mercy and compassion are linked. Joseph received God's compassion while in prison. Compassion can be defined as a feeling of deep sympathy and sorrow for another who is stricken by misfortune, accompanied by a strong desire to alleviate the suffering.

Psalm 86:15

But You, O Lord, are a God full of compassion, and gracious, long suffering and plenteous in mercy and truth.

Joseph's story reveals to us the compassionate heart of the Father. God is merciful and compassionate to the afflicted. Joseph would not be overlooked, instead God would intervene in his situation and eventually deliver him from the prison.

The scriptures reveal God's compassion on the prisoners. The prison is a symbol of oppression and bondage. Jesus came to open the prison. God does not despise the prisoners.

Psalm 69:33

For the Lord heareth the poor, and despiseth not his prisoners.

God hears the sighing and groaning of the prisoners and looses them.

Psalm 79:11
Let the sighing of the prisoner come before thee; according to the greatness of thy power preserve thou those that are appointed to die;

Psalm 102:20
To hear the groaning of the prisoner; to loose those that are appointed to death;

Psalm 146:7
Which executeth judgment for the oppressed: which giveth food to the hungry. The Lord looseth the prisoners:

It is estimated that Joseph spent approximately 13 years in Potiphar's house and in prison. Joseph was thirty years of age when he stood before Pharaoh (Gen. 41:46). Joseph was only seventeen when he was sold by his brothers (Gen. 37:2).

Dream Interpretation

Not only is a Joseph a dreamer, but he also interprets dreams. Pharaoh's butler and baker are im-
prisoned and placed in the care of Joseph. They
both dream. Joseph sees their sadness and asks
them why. They respond that they are troubled by
their dreams. Joseph then interprets their dreams.

Genesis 40:8-13
*And they said unto him, We have dreamed a
dream, and there is no interpreter of it. And Joseph
said unto them, Do not interpretations belong to
God? tell me them, I pray you.*

*And the chief butler told his dream to Joseph, and
said to him, In my dream, behold, a vine was before me;*

*And in the vine were three branches: and it was as
though it budded, and her blossoms shot forth;
and the clusters thereof brought forth ripe grapes:*

*And Pharaoh's cup was in my hand: and I took the
grapes, and pressed them into Pharaoh's cup, and
I gave the cup into Pharaoh's hand.*

*And Joseph said unto him, This is the interpretation
of it: The three branches are three days:*

*Yet within three days shall Pharaoh lift up thine
head, and restore thee unto thy place: and thou
shalt deliver Pharaoh's cup into his hand, after the
former manner when thou wast his butler.*

Joseph declares his innocence and asks the Butler to remember him by making mention of him to Pharaoh. The chief butler was restored to his position.

Genesis 40:14-15

But think on me when it shall be well with thee, and shew kindness, I pray thee, unto me, and make mention of me unto Pharaoh, and bring me out of this house:

For indeed I was stolen away out of the land of the Hebrews: and here also have I done nothing that they should put me into the dungeon.

The interpretation of the chief bakers dream was not good. The chief baker would be hanged by Pharaoh. The chief butler did not remember Joseph. It was still not the time for Joseph's dream to come to pass. Both Joseph and Jesus were with two others condemned to die, one of which was pardoned and given life.

Genesis 40:23

Yet did not the chief butler remember Joseph, but forgat him.

Joseph remained in the prison. Can you imagine his disappointment? Joseph, however, was not forgotten by God. The word of the Lord would test Joseph and refine him.

Cortni Marrazzo states, "Joseph's life was filled with what seemed to be setbacks on the surface, but in fact were the very situations that matured him, tested him, and ultimately set him up for God's plan to be manifested through him. In one of these major setbacks, we see the true, noble character that was the core of who Joseph was. After being wrongfully charged for an offense he did not commit, Joseph found himself in prison. One day he received two new cell mates, Pharaoh's chief baker and his chief cup-bearer. Since Joseph was responsible and skilled, he was ultimately placed in charge of these two prisoners. Having this kind of authority, Joseph could have easily lorded it over them and been rude and disrespectful. Instead, we see that Joseph was kind and compassionate to them, acknowledging their feelings and reaching out to them."

(Joseph in the Bible: 3 Things You Didn't Know About His Life & Story, crosswalk.com)

Pharaoh's Dreams

If there be a messenger with him, an inter-preter, one among a thousand, to shew unto man his uprightness. (Job 33:23)

There are four dreams mentioned in connection to Joseph. Pharaoh's dream is the fourth after Joseph, the butler, and the baker. God speaks in dreams. These dreams often need to be interpreted and interpreters are not common. Job calls them one among a thousand. None of the magicians in Egypt could interpret the dream. Joseph would be the only one with the interpretation.

Two years after Joseph interpreted the dreams for the cupbearer and the baker, Pharaoh had a dream. He was standing by the Nile when out of the river comes seven beautiful, healthy cows that begin grazing among the reeds. After that, seven other cows, gaunt and mangy, come up out of the Nile and stand beside the healthy cows on the riverbank. And the seven cows that were gaunt and unhealthy ate up the seven healthy cows. Pharaoh then woke up. He fell asleep again and had a second dream. Seven heads of grain, healthy and good, were growing on a single stalk. After them, seven other heads of grain sprouted, thin and scorched by the wind. The thin heads of grain swallowed up the seven healthy heads of grain. Then Pharaoh woke up again.
(Bibleblender.com)

Genesis 41:8-14

And it came to pass in the morning that his spirit was troubled; and he sent and called for all the magicians of Egypt, and all the wise men thereof: and Pharaoh told them his dream; but there was none that could interpret them unto Pharaoh.

Then spake the chief butler unto Pharaoh, saying, I do remember my faults this day:

Pharaoh was wroth with his servants, and put me in ward in the captain of the guard's house, both me and the chief baker:

And we dreamed a dream in one night, I and he; we dreamed each man according to the interpretation of his dream.

And there was there with us a young man, an Hebrew, servant to the captain of the guard; and we told him, and he interpreted to us our dreams; to each man according to his dream he did interpret.

And it came to pass, as he interpreted to us, so it was; me he restored unto mine office, and him he hanged.

Then Pharaoh sent and called Joseph, and they brought him hastily out of the dungeon: and he shaved himself, and changed his raiment, and came in unto Pharaoh.

The butler remembered Joseph from the prison. Joseph was of no value to him after he interpreted his dream, but now Joseph becomes valuable again because of his ability. The butler recognized his fault in forgetting Joseph.

Joseph interprets the dream. The dream was a revelation of what was coming upon the land:
Seven years of plenty followed by seven years of famine.

Genesis 41:25-32

And Joseph said unto Pharaoh, The dream of Pharaoh is one: God hath shewed Pharaoh what he is about to do.

The seven good kine are seven years; and the seven good ears are seven years: the dream is one.

And the seven thin and ill favoured kine that came up after them are seven years; and the seven empty ears blasted with the east wind shall be seven years of famine.

This is the thing which I have spoken unto Pharaoh: What God is about to do he sheweth unto Pharaoh.

Behold, there come seven years of great plenty throughout all the land of Egypt:

And there shall arise after them seven years of famine; and all the plenty shall be forgotten in the land of Egypt; and the famine shall consume the land;

And the plenty shall not be known in the land by reason of that famine following; for it shall be very grievous.
And for that the dream was doubled unto Pharaoh twice; it is because the thing is established by God, and God will shortly bring it to pass.

This interpretation undoubtedly stunned Pharaoh. He was furthermore stunned by Joseph's ability to interpret the dreams. God was revealing to Pharaoh the future of the nation.

Joseph's Counsel

Genesis 41:33-37

Now therefore let Pharaoh look out a man discreet and wise, and set him over the land of Egypt.

Let Pharaoh do this, and let him appoint officers over the land, and take up the fifth part of the land of Egypt in the seven plenteous years.

And let them gather all the food of those good years that come, and lay up corn under the hand of Pharaoh, and let them keep food in the cities.

And that food shall be for store to the land against the seven years of famine, which shall be in the land of Egypt; that the land perish not through the famine.

And the thing was good in the eyes of Pharaoh, and in the eyes of all his servants.

Pharaoh recognized the Spirit of God in Joseph. The spirit of wisdom is a manifestation of the Spirit of God. Joseph was the wisest man in Egypt.

Genesis 41:38-40

And Pharaoh said unto his servants, Can we find such a one as this is, a man in whom the Spirit of God is?

And Pharaoh said unto Joseph, Forasmuch as God hath shewed thee all this, there is none so discreet and wise as thou art:

Thou shalt be over my house, and according unto thy word shall all my people be ruled: only in the throne will I be greater than thou.

Promotion

Joseph is made the ruler of Egypt. He goes from the prison to ruling in Egypt suddenly. This is one of the most amazing promotions in all of scripture. Joseph's dream is now being fulfilled.

Genesis 41:41-46

And Pharaoh said unto Joseph, See, I have set thee over all the land of Egypt.

And Pharaoh took off his ring from his hand, and put it upon Joseph's hand, and arrayed him in vestures of fine linen, and put a gold chain about his neck;

And he made him to ride in the second chariot which he had; and they cried before him, Bow the knee: and he made him ruler over all the land of Egypt.

And Pharaoh said unto Joseph, I am Pharaoh, and without thee shall no man lift up his hand or foot in all the land of Egypt.

And Pharaoh called Joseph's name Zaphnath-paaneah; and he gave him to wife Asenath the daughter of Potipherah priest of On. And Joseph went out over all the land of Egypt.

And Joseph was thirty years old when he stood before Pharaoh king of Egypt. And Joseph went out from the presence of Pharaoh, and went throughout all the land of Egypt.

Joseph received a ring, a gold chain, and new apparel. He lost the robe given to him by his father in Egypt. He left his garment in the hand of Potiphar's wife when fleeing from her advances, but now He is clothed in fine linen. This represents a new position and status. His life was forever changed. Joseph is elevated to a position of high honor; His promotion came from God. Joseph is exalted, and set over all Egypt (Gen. 41:39-40); as God highly exalted Jesus (1 Peter 3:22; Philippians 2:5-11).

Zaphnathpaaneah is the name which Pharaoh gave to Joseph when he raised him to the rank of prime minister or grand vizier of the kingdom (Genesis 41:45). This is a pure Egyptian word, and has been variously explained. Some think it means "creator" or "preserver of life." Brugsch interprets it as "governor of the district of the place of life", i.e., of Goshen, the chief city of which was Pithom, "the place of life." Others explain it as meaning "a revealer of secrets", or "the man to whom secrets are revealed."
(Biblestudytools.com)

Authority And Wisdom

We will now look at Joseph's wisdom. Pharaoh recognized this wisdom and placed him in charge of his rulers. Joseph was commissioned to teach Pharaoh's senators wisdom.

Joseph became the overseer of Egypt. He went from being overseer of Potiphar's house, to overseer of the prison, to overseer of a nation.

Psalm 105:20-22
The king sent and loosed him; even the ruler of the people, and let him go free.
He made him lord of his house, and ruler of all his substance:
To bind his princes at his pleasure; and teach his senators wisdom.

The CEV Translation says, "Joseph was in command of the officials, and he taught the leaders how to use wisdom."

There is simply no substitute for wisdom. Wisdom is the principal thing (Prov. 4:7). There is no doubt that Joseph grew in wisdom over the years he served in Egypt before he met Pharaoh. He had acquired the wisdom to be a ruler in Egypt, a quality essential to ruling and decreeing justice.

Proverbs 8:15
By me kings reign, and princes decree justice.

Wisdom promotes and brings you to honor.

Proverbs 4:8
Exalt her, and she shall promote thee: she shall bring thee to honour, when thou dost embrace her.

Wisdom will preserve you.

Proverbs 4:6
Forsake her not, and she shall preserve thee: love her, and she shall keep thee.

Wisdom is connected to the fear of the Lord.

Proverbs 1:7
*The fear of the Lord is the beginning of knowledge: but fools despise **wisdom** and instruction.*

Wisdom is a key to happiness.

Proverbs 3:13
*Happy is the man that findeth **wisdom**, and the man that getteth understanding.*

Wisdom is better than money. Joseph gave a Pharaoh wisdom after interpreting his dream.

Proverbs 8:11

For **wisdom** *is better than rubies; and all the things that may be desired are not to be compared to it.*

Famine

And the seven years of plenteousness, that was in the land of Egypt, were ended.

And the seven years of dearth began to come, according as Joseph had said: and the dearth was in all lands; but in all the land of Egypt there was bread.

And when all the land of Egypt was famished, the people cried to Pharaoh for bread: and Pharaoh said unto all the Egyptians, Go unto Joseph; what he saith to you, do.

And the famine was over all the face of the earth: and Joseph opened all the storehouses, and sold unto the Egyptians; and the famine waxed sore in the land of Egypt.

And all countries came into Egypt to Joseph for to buy corn; because that the famine was so sore in all lands.

The people were sent by Pharaoh to Joseph to buy bread during the famine. All the surrounding countries came to Egypt to buy corn. Egypt was the only nation that had the advantage of a dream interpreter. This shows us the power of dreams and interpretation.

Joseph's ten brethren come into Egypt to buy corn. They have no idea that their brother Joseph is in charge. They are in for a big surprise. God's plan would come to pass in spite of their hatred, envy, and jealousy. Joseph's dream is about to be fulfilled.

God uses a famine to bring Joseph's brethren to him. Famine can be a picture of judgment and the scriptures have a lot to say about famine. Joseph has more than enough corn, he is not experiencing famine.

Genesis 42:1-3

Now when Jacob saw that there was corn in Egypt, Jacob said unto his sons, Why do ye look one upon another?
And he said, Behold, I have heard that there is corn in Egypt: get you down thither, and buy for us from thence; that we may live, and not die.
And Joseph's ten brethren went down to buy corn in Egypt.

Joseph's brethren come into Egypt and bow before Joseph. Joseph recognized his brethren, but he made himself strange to them. His brethren did not recognize him.

Joseph remembered the dreams he had dreamed about his brethren. Joseph speaks roughly to them and accuses them of being spies. They of course are not spies.

Genesis 42:6-7

And Joseph was the governor over the land, and he it was that sold to all the people of the land: and Joseph's brethren came, and bowed down themselves before him with their faces to the earth.

And Joseph saw his brethren, and he knew them, but made himself strange unto them, and spake roughly unto them; and he said unto them, Whence come ye? And they said, From the land of Canaan to buy food.

Genesis 42:8-9

And Joseph knew his brethren, but they knew not him.

And Joseph remembered the dreams which he dreamed of them, and said unto them, Ye are spies; to see the nakedness of the land ye are come.

Joseph's brethren are forced into this position due to famine. The righteous are promised satisfaction during famine (Psalm 37:19). The wicked are not satisfied during famine, God called for this famine (Psalm 105:16). Joseph's family would suffer from famine due to their mistreatment of Joseph. The righteous will not be careful in the year of drought (Jer. 17:8). The Lord satisfies the soul of the righteous in drought (Isa. 58:11).

Brokenness, Repentance, Forgiveness and Reconciliation

Although Joseph would eventually forgive and release his brethren from their wickedness, he did not do it immediately. Joseph was clever in dealing with his brethren. His brethren needed to be humbled, and think about what they had done.

Joseph made himself strange to them and spoke harshly to them. He accused them of being spies, and put them in prison for three days. He then asked about his younger brother who was not with them. His brethren were reminded of what they had done after experiencing these things. They knew that they were reaping from their ungodly act.

Genesis 42:21-22
And they said one to another, We are verily guilty concerning our brother, in that we saw the anguish of his soul, when he besought us, and we would not hear; therefore is this distress come upon us.
And Reuben answered them, saying, Spake I not unto you, saying, Do not sin against the child; and ye would not hear? therefore, behold, also his blood is required.

Joseph then ordered Simeon to remain in Egypt while they returned to Canaan to get Benjamin. Why did Joseph single out Simeon? Some had concluded that Simeon, the second oldest, was likely the ringleader of the plot to kill him. This would surely convince the brothers that they were being punished for their wicked deeds years earlier.

Joseph then put the silver they used to purchase the grain in their bags. This caused them more fear.

Genesis 42:27-28

And as one of them opened his sack to give his ass provender in the inn, he espied his money; for, behold, it was in his sack's mouth.

And he said unto his brethren, My money is restored; and, lo, it is even in my sack: and their heart failed them, and they were afraid, saying one to another, What is this that God hath done unto us?

When they returned home and told their father Jacob that Simeon was held in Egypt until Benjamin could be brought, Jacob refused. Simeon was held in Egypt for over a year. He had plenty of time to think about his misdeeds. Jacob had to eventually relent and allow Benjamin to return to Egypt with his brethren after they ran out of grain. When the brothers returned to Egypt with Benjamin, Joseph still refused to reveal his true identity (Genesis 43:15-16). They were welcomed to Joseph's house for dinner and bowed themselves again. When they were seated to dine at Joseph's house the eleven brothers were astonished to discover that

they were seated in perfect order according to age
(Genesis 43:33). Joseph then provides Benjamin
with more to eat than all the brethren. He is showing favor to Benjamin remembering that it was favor that caused his brothers to envy and hate him.

Joseph is not finished. A final act would bring them
to confession and repentance. Joseph had the
brothers' sacks filled with food to take back home
but he also had his personal silver cup put in Benjamin's bag. After the brothers left to travel home
Joseph sent men to catch up with them and ac-
cuse them of stealing the governor's cup. After the
cup was discovered in Benjamin's sack they returned to Egypt and threw themselves at Joseph's
feet. Joseph asked them why they stole his silver
cup (Genesis 44:1-15). Judah then responds:

Genesis 44:16
And Judah said, What shall we say unto my lord?
what shall we speak? or how shall we clear our-
selves? God hath found out the iniquity of thy ser-
vants: behold, we are my lord's servants, both we,
and he also with whom the cup is found.

Joseph's actions caused their sin to be exposed.
Joseph then threatened to arrest Benjamin. Judah
tells him that if they return home without Benjamin
that their father would surely die. Judah then offers
himself to spare Benjamin and his father. Judah
was the one that recommended selling Joseph instead of killing him. Judah suggested the idea of

selling his brother (Gen 37:26-28); the Greek name for Judah is Judas (Matt. 1:2-3). Judah admits his guilt and they were completely humbled and broken. Joseph did not reveal himself or offer forgiveness to his brethren until he saw humility and repentance. Joseph was finally satisfied and could no longer keep his identity from them. He began to weep.

Genesis 45:1-3
Then Joseph could not refrain himself before all them that stood by him; and he cried, Cause every man to go out from me. And there stood no man with him, while Joseph made himself known unto his brethren.

And he wept aloud: and the Egyptians and the house of Pharaoh heard.

And Joseph said unto his brethren, I am Joseph; doth my father yet live? And his brethren could not answer him; for they were troubled at his presence.

When Joseph revealed himself to his brethren, he was overwhelmed with love for them. Joseph extended forgiveness after he saw his brethren admit their wrong. He brothers were now speechless. Now, Joseph knew his beloved father was still alive.

Joseph had come to a realization that his coming into Egypt was his destiny and purpose. He knew that he had been sent by God. He had been sent to preserve and deliver his family. Joseph was instrumental in God's plan for Israel. Israel had to be preserved for Messiah to come.

Genesis 45:4-8

And Joseph said unto his brethren, Come near to me, I pray you. And they came near. And he said, I am Joseph your brother, whom ye sold into Egypt.
Now therefore be not grieved, nor angry with yourselves, that ye sold me hither: for God did send me before you to preserve life.
For these two years hath the famine been in the land: and yet there are five years, in the which there shall neither be earing nor harvest.
And God sent me before you to preserve you a posterity in the earth, and to save your lives by a great deliverance.
So now it was not you that sent me hither, but God: and he hath made me a father to Pharaoh, and lord of all his house, and a ruler throughout all the land of Egypt.

Joseph is reconciled with his brethren, harboring no unforgiveness or bitterness toward them. This is a great example of forgiveness and restoration.

Joseph tells his brethren not to be grieved. They had to be dealing with a tremendous amount of guilt and shame. They had to be embarrassed by their act of treachery towards Joseph, but he is releasing them from this burden.

Joseph had become a father to Pharaoh. Joseph has come from being the youngest brother to becoming a father. This speaks of growth and maturity in spite of his afflictions.

Joseph is a type of an apostle (a sent one). He is the picture of a pioneer, a pathfinder, a trailblazer. He was sent to prepare the way for others.

Joseph was blessed alone. He was separated from his family, and had to walk alone with God. He is like Abraham in this sense. God called Abraham alone and blessed him.

Isaiah 51:2
Look unto Abraham your father, and unto Sarah that bare you: for I called him alone, and blessed him, and increased him.

Genesis 49:22
Joseph is a fruitful bough, even a fruitful bough by a well; whose branches run over the wall:

Exodus 1:7
And the children of Israel were fruitful, and increased abundantly, and multiplied, and waxed exceeding mighty; and the land was filled with them.

The Lord God caused Joseph's vine to "climb over a wall" into Egypt, and God used him there. "God has made me fruitful in the land of my affliction" (Gen. 41:52). "God has made me lord of all Egypt" (Gen. 45:9).

The original mandate to Adam of multiplication and fruitfulness can be seen through Joseph, and eventually through Israel in Egypt (Gen. 47:27). Abraham's seed multiplies under Joseph. The Joseph story is the capstone of Genesis. What begins in Adam and Abraham is somewhat fulfilled through Joseph. Joseph is a picture of redemption, blessing, covenant, and ruling (kingdom). Joseph provides bread for the nations. Jesus is the bread of life. The ultimate fulfillment of God's covenant promises to Abraham come through Christ, who is the greater Joseph. Joseph saves his family from famine and preserves the Messianic line.

Genesis 49:24
*But his bow abode in strength, and the **arms** of his hands were made strong by the hands of the mighty God of Jacob; (from thence is the shepherd, the stone of Israel:)*

Will Pounds states, "Joseph's arms were made strong by the hands of the mighty God of Jacob." The image is that of the LORD God placing His strong hands upon the hands of Joseph as he draws the string of his bow just as a strong father might steady and guide his son in giving an archery lesson. Who steadies your hand? Who gives you inner strength? Joseph's "bow remained steady, his strong arms stayed limber, because of the hand of the Mighty One of Jacob." (Joseph's Secret To Success, www.abideinChrist.com)

Samuel Emadi states, "Jacob depicts the coming king from Judah with imagery that closely resembles Joseph's narrative. Judah's brothers will praise and even "bow down" before him—the same word used three times when the brothers bowed to Joseph in the dreams (Gen. 37:7, 9, 10) and another three times when they bowed before him in the Egyptian court (Gen. 42:4; 43:26, 28). Indeed, the image of 11 brothers "bowing" to their royal sibling in Genesis 49:8 reads like a summary of the preceding Joseph story. This similarity is deliberate. When we ask what the coming Messiah will look like, we have an answer provided in Jacob's words—he will look like Joseph." (What the Joseph Story Is Really About by Samuel Emadi, thegospelcoalition.org)

Genesis 50:20
But as for you, ye thought evil against me; but God meant it unto good, to bring to pass, as it is this day, to save much people alive.

Jacob Before Pharaoh

Genesis 47:7-9

And Joseph brought in Jacob his father, and set him before Pharaoh: and Jacob blessed Pharaoh. And Pharaoh said unto Jacob, How old art thou? And Jacob said unto Pharaoh, The days of the years of my pilgrimage are an hundred and thirty years: few and evil have the days of the years of my life been, and have not attained unto the days of the years of the life of my fathers in the days of their pilgrimage.

Jacob Calls his days "few and evil." Jacob would bless Pharaoh and Joseph's two sons. Jacob would die in Egypt, but request to be buried in Canaan.

Genesis 47:25

And they said, Thou hast saved our lives: let us find grace in the sight of my lord, and we will be Pharaoh's servants.

Joseph saved his brothers lives. Joseph is a savior. He is a type of our Savior Jesus Christ.

John and Paula Stevenson make these comparisons between Jacob and Joseph, and the actions of Jacob toward Esau, and Joseph's brethren toward Joseph:

"There are a number of contrasts and comparisons that we can see between Joseph and his father Jacob.

Jacob	Joseph
He was the youngest son	He was the youngest son
His name means "heel-grabber"	His name means "to add"
He was loved by his mother	He was loved by his Father
He bought the birthright from his brother	His father gave him the birthright over his older brothers
He was hated by his older brother	He was hated by his older brothers
As a result of his brother's threats, he traveled to Haran	As a result of his brother's plot, he was sold and taken to Eygpt
He works for Laban in Haran	He worked for Potiphar in Eygpt
Jacob brought prosperity to Laban	Joseph brought prosperity to Potiphar
Laban deceived Jacob	Potiphar was deceived his wife

When Jacob left Laban he was a rich man	Joseph left prison to become ruler of all of Egypt
Jacob became fearful as he anticipated meeting his brother again	His brothers became fearful when they met Joesph again
Jacob was eventually reconciled with his brother	Joseph was eventually reconciled with his brothers

There is a striking parallel here between the actions of Jacob's sons in deceiving their father and in Jacob's own actions some 30 years earlier when he deceived his own father.

Jacob deceived Isaac	Jacob's sons deceived him
Jacob had deliberately deceived Isaac into giving him the blessing	Jacob's sons deceived him into believing Joseph is dead
An article of clothing used in the deception: Jacob wraps his arms and his head in wool to simulate the hairy arms and back of Esau	An article of clothing used in deception: Joseph's brothers dip his tunic in blood to simulate Joseph's torn body

Jacob had deceived his father with the skin of a dead goat	Jacob's sons deceived him with the blood of a dead goat

(John and Paula Stevenson, Favored Son, Hated Brother, www.angelfire.com)

Joseph's Final Words to His Brethren

Genesis 50:14-21

And Joseph returned into Egypt, he, and his brethren, and all that went up with him to bury his father, after he had buried his father.

And when Joseph's brethren saw that their father was dead, they said, Joseph will peradventure hate us, and will certainly requite us all the evil which we did unto him.

And they sent a messenger unto Joseph, saying, Thy father did command before he died, saying,

So shall ye say unto Joseph, Forgive, I pray thee now, the trespass of thy brethren, and their sin; for they did unto thee evil: and now, we pray thee, forgive the trespass of the servants of the God of thy father. And Joseph wept when they spake unto him.

And his brethren also went and fell down before his face; and they said, Behold, we be thy servants.

And Joseph said unto them, Fear not: for am I in the place of God?

But as for you, ye thought evil against me; but God meant it unto good, to bring to pass, as it is this day, to save much people alive.

Now therefore fear ye not: I will nourish you, and your little ones. And he comforted them, and spake kindly unto them.

Joseph's brethren feared retribution from Joseph after the death of their father. They sent a message to Joseph from their father asking for his forgiveness. They come and bow down to Joseph, and say "we are your servants." The dream they hated had come to pass. Joseph weeps and assures them that they will be nourished and protected by him. What they meant for evil God meant unto good. Joseph offers forgiveness to his brethren, just like Jesus offered forgiveness to those who crucified him.

Hebrews 11:22
By faith Joseph, when he died, made mention of the departing of the children of Israel; and gave commandment concerning his bones.

Joseph knew that Egypt would not be the final resting place for Israel. God had promised Abraham the land of Canaan. God also revealed to Abraham that his descendants would be afflicted for many years in a strange land. It is possible that Abraham conveyed this to his children before his death.

Genesis 15:13
And he said unto Abram, Know of a surety that thy seed shall be a stranger in a land that is not theirs, and shall serve them; and they shall afflict them four hundred years;

Genesis 50:24-26

And Joseph said unto his brethren, I die: and God will surely visit you, and bring you out of this land unto the land which he sware to Abraham, to Isaac, and to Jacob.

And Joseph took an oath of the children of Israel, saying, God will surely visit you, and ye shall carry up my bones from hence.

So Joseph died, being an hundred and ten years old: and they embalmed him, and he was put in a coffin in Egypt.

God would visit Israel and bring them out of Egypt. This is another type of Christ visiting Israel and bringing (redeeming) them out of sin and death (Egypt). Egypt would become a symbol of Old Covenant Jerusalem and bondage to sin and the law (Rev. 11:8) Bones are synonymous with resurrection (Ezek. 37) Joseph was a believer in the resurrection, and the coming deliverer.

Hosea 11:1

When Israel was a child, then I loved him, and called my son out of Egypt.

Joseph may have known what was coming to his people in Egypt, but he also knew another deliverance was coming. The inheritance of Canaan is another picture of the kingdom, living in the land (prosperity and peace) under the rule of God. Joseph would come out of Egypt. Jesus would also come out of Egypt (the place of refuge). It is interesting that Joseph brought Jesus into and out of Egypt.

While only Jesus was truly sinless, Joseph is one of the few people significantly written about in the Bible of which no sins are mentioned. Joseph overcame temptation from Potiphar's wife, and Jesus overcame temptation in the wilderness. The story of a Joseph is a powerful witness of a Christ in the Old Testament.

The Word of the Lord Tested Him

Dreams and prophecy have a way of testing us. The delay in fulfillment can refine and purify us. We examine our hearts during these times and make appropriate adjustments that prepare us for the fulfillment.

Psalm 105:18-20
Whose feet they hurt with fetters: he was laid in iron:
Until the time that his word came: the word of the Lord tried him.
The king sent and loosed him; even the ruler of the people, and let him go free.

The Amplified translation says, "Until the time that his word (of prophecy regarding his brothers) came true. The word of the Lord tested and refined him."

Some translations say the word of the Lord purified him. We often need purification from pride, selfish ambition, bitterness, hurt, anger, selfishness, and vanity. Joseph's time in prison was a season of testing. His dream would test him, and Joseph would pass the test. The Voice translation says, "That was until the Eternal's promises came to pass: His word tested Joseph and proved him worthy."

Isaiah 48:10
Behold, I have refined thee, but not with silver; I have chosen thee in the furnace of affliction.

The ERV translation says, "Look, I will make you pure, but not in the way you make silver pure. I will make you pure by giving you troubles." Joseph was purified in the furnace of affliction. A furnace is used to separate the dross from the silver and gold. Trouble has a way of removing impurities from our lives.

Psalm 34:19
Many are the afflictions of the righteous: but the Lord delivereth him out of them all.

Affliction is connected to misery, wormwood, and gall. Wormwood and gall are pictures of bitterness.

Lamentations 3:19
Remembering mine affliction and my misery, the wormwood and the gall.

Bitterness is one of the major things that those who are afflicted must overcome. Joseph would have to be purged from any bitterness towards his brethren. This requires forgiveness.

Manasseh and Ephraim

Genesis 41:50-52

And unto Joseph were born two sons before the years of famine came, which Asenath the daughter of Potipherah priest of On bare unto him.

And Joseph called the name of the firstborn Manasseh: For God, said he, hath made me forget all my toil, and all my father's house.

And the name of the second called he Ephraim: For God hath caused me to be fruitful in the land of my affliction.

Joseph named his two sons after his experience in Egypt. His firstborn Manasseh is a sign that he can forget his toil in Egypt. This represents healing and restoration. His second son Ephraim reveals his fruitfulness and prosperity in the land of affliction. These two sons would later be included in the tribes of Israel. They represent a double portion. God gave Joseph double for his trouble.

Legacy and Blessings

Manasseh and Ephraim represent Joseph's legacy. Moses' prophecy over Joseph's descendants is full of blessing. Joseph would not only affect his generation, but generations to come. Your dream is not just for you. Your dream has a purpose that goes well beyond your lifetime.

Joseph's dream separated him from his family. Joseph is called the one who was separate from his brethren. Your dream is what distinguishes you and often separates you from others.

Deuteronomy 33:13-17
And of Joseph he said, Blessed of the Lord be his land, for the precious things of heaven, for the dew, and for the deep that coucheth beneath,
And for the precious fruits brought forth by the sun, and for the precious things put forth by the moon,
And for the chief things of the ancient mountains, and for the precious things of the lasting hills,
And for the precious things of the earth and fulness thereof, and for the good will of him that dwelt in the bush: let the blessing come upon the head of Joseph, and upon the top of the head of him that was separated from his brethren.
His glory is like the firstling of his bullock, and his horns are like the horns of unicorns: with them he shall push the people together to the ends of the

earth: and they are the ten thousands of Ephraim, and they are the thousands of Manasseh.

This prophecy speaks of Joseph's power, strength, and glory. Blessings would be upon the head of Joseph's descendants. The heavens, the deep, the sun, the moon, the mountains and the hills would release blessings.

We learn the providence of God in the life of Joseph. Joseph could not cause his dream to come to pass in his own strength. God caused his dream to come to pass. Joseph overcome impossible odds to come to a place of power and authority in Egypt. There is no way he could have accomplished this without the help of God. Joseph's glory and strength came from God.

Lessons from the Life of Joseph

26 Insights from the life of Joseph:

1. The pit, Potiphar's house, nor the prison could stop Joseph's dream from coming to pass.

2. The jealousy and hatred of Joseph's brethren drove him into his destiny.

3. Joseph's integrity in Potiphar's house and the prison opened the way for him to arrive at the palace.

4. Jospeh was separated from his brethren. Sometimes separation is necessary to walk in your destiny.

5. Joseph's character was the opposite of the wickedness of his brethren. His character made them uncomfortable.

6. Joseph recognized his brethren when they came to Egypt, but they did not recognize him. He was not the same person they sold as a slave.

7. The chief butler forgot Joseph in the prison, but God did not forget him. Man may forget you, but God knows where you are.

8. God gave Joseph favor in the prison. Favor will work for you in the worst places.

9. Joseph was hurt by his brethren. Sometimes hurt is a part of walking in your destiny.

10. Joseph met the chief butler in prison and interpreted his dream. This meeting was his connection to the palace. You can have a divine connection even in the prison.

11. Pharaoh needed someone to interpret his dream. He located Joseph in the prison. People who need you will find you.

12. Potiphar's wife lied on Joseph and had him put in prison. Those who have great destiny will have to endure lies.

13. Potiphar's wife wanted to sleep with Joseph. Sexual temptation will come to those with great destiny.

14. Potiphar trusted Joseph with his entire house, including his wife. Can you be trusted?

15. Joseph had to be patient while being stuck in prison. Patience in necessary if you are to arrive at the palace.

16. Jacob favored Joseph and gave him a coat of many colors. Joseph's brethren were jealous. Favor will attract jealousy.

17. Joseph had two sons in Egypt, Manasseh and Ephraim. God will give you double for your trouble.

18. Joseph was a deliverer for his family. You may be the key to deliverance for those who mistreated you.

19. Jospeh's father thought he was dead. You will not die, but live and fulfill your destiny.

20. Joseph's wisdom preserved him. He used that wisdom to counsel Pharaoh. Wisdom will be necessary to arrive at the palace.

21. Joseph dreamed that his brethren would bow down to him. They hated the dream. They could not see themselves under Joseph. Your destiny will challenge the pride of your brethren.

22. Joseph said **"no"** to Potiphar's wife. You must learn to say **"no"** to some people if you want to arrive at the palace.

23. Joseph was **sen**t by God into Egypt to prepare the way for his family. People who mistreat you do not realize you are being **sent**.

24. Joseph's brethren were afraid when they saw Joseph in Egypt. Joseph did not repay them with evil. He understood what they had meant for evil, God had turned it around for their good.

25. The pit and the prison were the low places in Joseph's life. They represent **humility**. Before honor and promotion is **humility**.

26. Joseph's gift (interpreting dreams) was a key to his arriving at the palace. Don't despise your gift.

Made in the USA
San Bernardino, CA
03 August 2020

76417330R00044